the
sea
365 reflections

An Hachette UK Company
www.hachette.co.uk

First published in Great Britain in 2019 by Pyramid,
an imprint of Octopus Publishing Group Ltd
Carmelite House
50 Victoria Embankment
London EC4Y 0DZ
www.octopusbooks.co.uk

ISBN 978-0-7537-3359-2

A CIP catalogue record for this book is available from the British Library

Printed and bound in China

10 9 8 7 6 5 4 3 2 1

Publisher: Lucy Pessell
Designer: Lisa Layton
Editor: Sarah Vaughan
Contributing Editor: Anna Bowles
Production Manager: Lisa Pinnell

the
sea
365 reflections

*L*ook at that sea, girls—
all silver and shadow
and vision of things not
seen. We couldn't enjoy its
loveliness any more if we
had millions of dollars and
ropes of diamonds.

Lucy Maud Montgomery,
Anne of Green Gables

from "God Moves in a Mysterious Way"

God moves in a mysterious way,
His wonders to perform;
He plants his footsteps in the sea,
And rides upon the storm.

William Cowper

The Norse believed there were nine spirits of the sea waves. They were the daughters of Aegir the sea god and his wife Rán.

Far out in the ocean, where the water is as blue as the prettiest cornflower, and as clear as crystal, it is very, very deep; so deep, indeed, that no cable could fathom it: many church steeples, piled one upon another, would not reach from the ground beneath to the surface of the water above. There dwell the Sea King and his subjects.

Hans Christian Andersen, *The Little Mermaid*

Come O'Er the Sea

Come o'er the sea,
Maiden with me,
Mine through sunshine, storm, and snows;
Seasons may roll,
But the true soul
Burns the same, where'er it goes.
Let fate frown on, so we love and part not;
'Tis life where thou art, 'tis death were thou are not.
Then come o'er the sea,
Maiden with me,
Come wherever the wild wind blows;
Seasons may roll,
But the true soul
Burns the same, where'er it goes.

Was not the sea
Made for the Free,
Land for courts and chains alone?
Here we are slaves,
But, on the waves,
Love and Liberty's all our own.
No eye to watch, and no tongue to wound us
All earth forgot, and all heaven around us—
Then come o'er the sea,
Maiden, with me,
Mine through sunshine, storms, and snows
Seasons may roll,
But the true soul
Burns the same, where'er it goes.

Thomas Moore

$\mathcal{E}$very time we walk along a beach some ancient urge disturbs us so that we find ourselves shedding shoes and garments or scavenging among seaweed and whitened timbers like the homesick refugees of a long war.

Loren Eiseley, *The Unexpected Universe*

Life is as inexorable as the sea.

Thomas Wentworth Higginson, *A Moonglade*

from "The Sea and the Hills"

Who hath desired the Sea?—the sight of salt water unbounded—
The heave and the halt and the hurl and the crash of the comber wind-hounded?

William Cowper

When anxious, uneasy and bad thoughts come, I go to the sea, and the sea drowns them out with its great wide sounds, cleanses me with its noise, and imposes a rhythm upon everything in me that is bewildered and confused.

Rainer Maria Rilke, Letter to Clara Rilke, March 27, 1903

The blue colour of the sea is the result of the sun's red and orange wavelengths being absorbed by the surface and its blue wavelengths penetrating deeper.

There is nothing like lying flat on your back on the deck, alone except for the helmsman aft at the wheel, silence except for the lapping of the sea against the side of the ship. At that time you can be equal to Ulysses and brother to him.

Errol Flynn, actor

Once I sat upon a promontory,
And heard a mermaid, on a dolphin's back,
Uttering such dulcet and harmonious breath,
That the rude sea grew civil at her song,
And certain stars shot madly from their spheres
To hear the sea-maid's music.

William Shakespeare, A Midsummer Night's Dream

from "The White Ship"

The sea hath no king but God alone...

Dante Gabriel Rossetti

In Hawaiian mythology, Kanaloa was the god of the ocean and the ocean winds. He was feared as much as worshipped, and sometimes pictured as an evil black squid. When old Hawaiians built a canoe they would invoke the blessing of Kane the creator god for the building and Kanaloa's for its sailing.

Don't go mooning after the stars,
when the wide sea is all around you.
It's a sky of its own, you know.

Robin Hobb, *Ship of Destiny*

Being out there in the ocean, God's creation, it's like a gift He has given us to enjoy.

Bethany Hamilton, professional surfer

Those who live by the sea can hardly form a single thought of which the sea would not be part.

Hermann Broch, *The Spell*

But more wonderful than the lore of old men and the lore of books is the secret lore of ocean. Blue, green, gray, white or black; smooth, ruffled, or mountainous; that ocean is not silent. All my days have I watched it and listened to it, and I know it well. At first it told to me only the plain little tales of calm beaches and near ports, but with the years it grew more friendly and spoke of other things; of things more strange and more distant in space and time. Sometimes at twilight the gray vapors of the horizon have parted to grant me glimpses of the ways beyond; and sometimes at night the deep waters of the sea have grown clear and phosphorescent, to grant me glimpses of the ways beneath. And these glimpses have been as often of the ways that were and the ways that might be, as of the ways that are; for ocean is more ancient than the mountains, and freighted with the memories and the dreams of Time.

H. P. Lovecraft, *The White Ship*

from "A Life Drama"

The sea complains upon a thousand shores.

Alexander Smith

The sea is everything.
It covers seven tenths
of the terrestrial globe.
Its breath is pure and
healthy. It is an immense
desert, where man is
never lonely, for he feels
life stirring on all sides.

Jules Verne,
20,000 Leagues Under the Sea

The Maori of New Zealand believed that Tangaroa, god of the sea, was in constant strife with Tāne, the god of forests. When they ventured out to sea, the Maori were representatives of Tāne venturing into Tangaroa's realm, so it was important to make offerings before setting out.

I love the sea's sounds and the way it reflects the sky. The colours that shimmer across its surface are unbelievable. This, combined with the colour of the water over white sand, surprises me every time.

John Dyer, painter

from "The Secret of the Sea"

Like the long waves on a sea-beach,
  Where the sand as silver shines,
With a soft, monotonous cadence,
  Flow its unrhymed lyric lines;—

Telling how the Count Arnaldos,
  With his hawk upon his hand,
Saw a fair and stately galley,
  Steering onward to the land;—

How he heard the ancient helmsman
  Chant a song so wild and clear,
That the sailing sea-bird slowly
  Poised upon the mast to hear,

Till his soul was full of longing,
  And he cried, with impulse strong,—
"Helmsman! for the love of heaven,
  Teach me, too, that wondrous song!"

"Wouldst thou,"—so the helmsman answered,
  "Learn the secret of the sea?
Only those who brave its dangers
  Comprehend its mystery!"

In each sail that skims the horizon,
  In each landward-blowing breeze,
I behold that stately galley,
  Hear those mournful melodies;

Till my soul is full of longing
  For the secret of the sea,
And the heart of the great ocean
  Sends a thrilling pulse through me.

Henry Wadsworth Longfellow

$\mathscr{A}$ll morning under a milky sky the waters in the bay had swelled and swelled, rising to unheard-of heights, the small waves creeping over parched sand that for years had known no wetting save for rain and lapping the very bases of the dunes. The rusted hulk of the freighter that had run aground at the far end of the bay longer ago than any of us could remember must have thought it was being granted a relaunch. I would not swim again, after that day.

John Banville, *The Sea*

Tides are caused by the effect of the Sun and the Moon. As the Earth turns, the Sun's and Moon's gravity pulls on the water in the oceans.

No literature is richer than that of the sea. No story is more enthralling, no tradition is more secure.

Felix Riesenberg, maritime officer and writer

from "Sea Fever"

I must go down to the seas again, to the lonely sea and the sky,
And all I ask is a tall ship and a star to steer her by;
And the wheel's kick and the wind's song and the white sail's shaking,
And a grey mist on the sea's face, and a grey dawn breaking.

John Masefield

I would not creep along the coast but steer
Out in mid-sea, by guidance of the stars.

George Eliot, *Middlemarch*

The Sound of the Sea

The sea awoke at midnight from its sleep,
And round the pebbly beaches far and wide
I heard the first wave of the rising tide
Rush onward with uninterrupted sweep;
A voice out of the silence of the deep,
A sound mysteriously multiplied
As of a cataract from the mountain's side,
Or roar of winds upon a wooded steep.
So comes to us at times, from the unknown
And inaccessible solitudes of being,
The rushing of the sea-tides of the soul;
And inspirations, that we deem our own,
Are some divine of foreshadowing and foreseeing
Of things beyond our reason or control.

Henry Wadsworth Longfellow

The voice of the sea
speaks to the soul.
The touch of the sea
is sensuous, enfolding
the body in its soft,
close embrace.

Kate Chopin, *The Awakening*

How suggestive
the sounds of the
thunder of waves upon
rocks and headlands
in a storm. They seem
to fill the soul with the
noblest of all music.
I know nothing more
exciting than a storm
at sea.

Henry James Slack,
The Ministry of the Beautiful

As If the Sea Should Part

As if the Sea should part
And show a further Sea—
And that—a further—and the Three
But a presumption be—

Of Periods of Seas—
Unvisited of Shores—
Themselves the Verge of Seas to be—
Eternity—is Those—

Emily Dickinson

The wind and the waves are always on the side of the ablest navigator.

Edmund Gibbon, historian

The Greek god Poseidon was considered to be moody by nature, with an unstable temperament. His violent rages resulted in storms and tsunamis.

There is indeed, perhaps, no better way to hold communion with the sea than sitting in the sun on the veranda of a fishermen's cafe.

Lisa Wingate,
The Shores of Moses Lake

The sea pronounces something, over and over, in a hoarse whisper; I cannot quite make it out.

Annie Dillard, *Teaching a Stone to Talk*

You could start now, and spend another forty years learning about the sea without running out of new things to know.

Peter Benchley, *The Deep*

With Ships the Sea was Sprinkled

With ships the sea was sprinkled far and nigh,
Like stars in heaven, and joyously it showed;
Some lying fast at anchor in the road,
Some veering up and down, one knew not why.
A goodly vessel did I then espy
Come like a giant from a haven broad;
And lustily along the bay she strode,
Her tackling rich, and of apparel high.
The ship was nought to me, nor I to her,
Yet I pursued her with a lover's look;
This ship to all the rest did I prefer:
When will she turn, and whither? She will brook
No tarrying; where she comes the winds must stir:
On went she, and due north her journey took.

William Wordsworth

As for me, I am tormented with an everlasting itch for things remote. I love to sail forbidden seas, and land on barbarous coasts.

Herman Melville, *Moby Dick*

Waves are the voices of tides. Tides are life.

Tamora Pierce, writer

Follow the river
and you will
find the sea.

French Proverb

A person should go out on the water
on a fine day to a small distance
from a beautiful coast, if he would see
Nature really smile. Never does she look
so delightful, as when the sun is brightly
reflected by the water, while the waves are
gently rippling, and the prospect receives
life and animation from the glancing
transit of an occasional row-boat, and the
quieter motion of a few small vessels. But
the land must be well in sight; not only for
its own sake, but because the immensity
and awfulness of a mere sea-view would
ill accord with the other parts of the
glittering and joyous scene.

Augustus William Hare and Julius Charles Hare,
Guesses at Truth, by Two Brothers

Even if you never have the chance to see or touch the ocean, the ocean touches you with every breath you take, every drop of water you drink, every bite you consume. Everyone, everywhere is inextricably connected to and utterly dependent upon the existence of the sea.

Sylvia Earle,
The World is Blue: How Our Fate and the Oceans are One

How inappropriate to call this planet
Earth when it is clearly Ocean.

Arthur C. Clarke, science writer

After the Sea-ship

After the Sea-Ship—after the whistling winds;
After the white-gray sails, taut to their spars and ropes,
Below, a myriad, myriad waves, hastening, lifting up their necks,
Tending in ceaseless flow toward the track of the ship:
Waves of the ocean, bubbling and gurgling, blithely prying,
Waves, undulating waves—liquid, uneven, emulous waves,
Toward that whirling current, laughing and buoyant, with curves,
Where the great Vessel, sailing and tacking, displaced the surface;
Larger and smaller waves, in the spread of the ocean, yearnfully
   flowing;
The wake of the Sea-Ship, after she passes—flashing and frolicsome,
   under the sun,
A motley procession, with many a fleck of foam, and many fragments,
Following the stately and rapid Ship—in the wake following.

Walt Whitman

The ocean is alive with sounds, and the most impressive are those made by whales. Not only is whale song hauntingly beautiful, but those on the lowest frequencies can travel up to 16,000 kilometres (10,000 miles) through the water.

The sea refreshes our imagination because it does not make us think of human life; yet it rejoices the soul, because, like the soul, it is an infinite and impotent striving, a strength that is ceaselessly broken by falls, an eternal and exquisite lament. The sea thus enchants us like music, which, unlike language, never bears the traces of things, never tells us anything about human beings, but imitates the stirrings of the soul. Sweeping up with the waves of those movements, plunging back with them, the heart thus forgets its own failures and finds solace in an intimate harmony between its own sadness and the sea's sadness, which merges the sea's destiny with the destinies of all things.

Marcel Proust, *Regrets, Reveries, the Colour of Time*

from "Exiled"

Searching my heart for its true sorrow,
This is the thing I find to be:
That I am weary of words and people,
Sick of the city, wanting the sea.

Edna St. Vincent Millay

The sea god Tam Kung, worshipped in Hong Kong, is said to have the ability to predict the weather.

An amazing 95 percent of the ocean remains unexplored by humans.

She had thought the open sea would be flat, like a mirror or a coin. But it had colours and shapes, turning green or black under approaching storm. Sometimes it was red and purple and silver and white gold. It had sharp hedges. It had its tempers, its blue spells, its fits of laughter.

Jennifer Zeynab Joukhadar, *The Map of Salt and Stars*

Ocean people are different from land people. The ocean never stops saying and asking into ears, which don't sleep like eyes. Those who live by the sea examine the driftwood and glass balls that float from foreign ships. They let scores of invisible imps loose out of found bottles. In a scoop of salt water, they revive the dead blobs that have been beached in storms and tides: fins, whiskers, and gills unfold; mouths, eyes, and colours bloom and spread. Sometimes ocean people are given to understand the newness and oldness of the world; then all morning they try to keep that boundless joy like a little sun inside their chests. The ocean also makes its people know immensity.

Maxine Hong Kingston, *China Men*

*L*imitless and immortal, the waters are the beginning and end of all things on earth.

Heinrich Zimmer,
Myths and Symbols in Indian Art and Civilisation

I t is said that the magical island of Avalon once existed off the south or west coast of Britain, only to sink into the waves. Arthurian legend states that the Lady of the Lake lived in Avalon, and that King Arthur was buried there.

I spent uncounted hours sitting
at the bow looking at the water
and the sky, studying each
wave, different from the last,
seeing how it caught the light,
the air, the wind; watching
patterns, the sweep of it all,
and letting it take me. The sea.

Gary Paulsen, *Caught by the Sea: My Life on Boats*

from "Young Sea"

The sea speaks
And only the stormy hearts
Know what it says:
It is the face
of a rough mother speaking.

Carl Sandburg

I couldn't imagine living in a state that didn't reach the ocean. It was a giant reset button. You could go to the edge of the land and see infinity and feel renewed.

Avery Sawyer, *Notes to Self*

She loves the serene
brutality of the ocean,
loves the electric
power she felt with
each breath of wet,
briny air.

Holly Black, *Tithe*

The Sea Spirit

I smile o'er the wrinkled blue¬
Lo! the sea is fair,
Smooth as the flow of a maiden's hair;
And the welkin's light shines through
Into mid-sea caverns of beryl hue,
And the little waves laugh and the mermaids sing,
And the sea is a beautiful, sinuous thing!

I scowl in sullen guise¬
The sea grows dark and dun,
The swift clouds hide the sun
But not the bale-light in my eyes,
And the frightened wind as it flies
Ruffles the billows with stormy wing,
And the sea is a terrible, treacherous thing!

When moonlight glimmers dim
I pass in the path of the mist,
Like a pale spirit by spirits kissed.
At dawn I chant my own weird hymn,
And I dabble my hair in the sunset's rim,
And I call to the dwellers along the shore
With a voice of gramarye evermore.

And if one for love of me
Gives to my call an ear,
I will woo him and hold him dear,
And teach him the way of the sea,
And my glamor shall ever over him be;
Though he wander afar in the cities of men
He will come at last to my arms again.

Lucy Maud Montgomery

Afterwards violent earthquakes and floods took place; and in a single day and night… the island of Atlantis vanished into the depths of the sea. For this reason, the sea in those parts is impassable and impenetrable, because there is a shoal of mud in the way, thrown up by the subsidence of the island.

Plato, *Timaeus*, the first recorded mention of Atlantis

I love the sea's sounds and the way it reflects the sky. The colours that shimmer across its surface are unbelievable. This, combined with the colour of the water over white sand, surprises me every time.

John Dyer, poet

The Bermuda Triangle is a 700,000-square-kilometre (270,000-square-mile) area of sea in the Atlantic Ocean where over a thousand ships and planes have disappeared since records began. Various explanations have been offered, including aliens and sea monsters, but scientists' latest theory is that the disappearances are caused by rogue waves. If storms come in from the north, south and west at the same time, waves up to 30 metres (98 feet) high may be generated.

Twelve people have visited the Moon, but just three have been to the Challenger Deep, the deepest part of the ocean.

The sea lives in every one of us.

Wyland, artist

I could never stay long enough on the shore; the tang of the untainted, fresh, and free sea air was like a cool, quieting thought.

Helen Keller, *The Story of My Life*

Beyond the Sea

Beyond the sea, beyond the sea,
My heart is gone, far, far from me;
And ever on its track will flee
My thoughts, my dreams, beyond the sea.

Beyond the sea, beyond the sea,
The swallow wanders fast and free:
Oh, happy bird! were I like thee,
I, too, would fly beyond the sea.

Beyond the sea, beyond the sea,
Are kindly hearts and social glee:
But here for me they may not be;
My heart is gone beyond the sea.

Thomas Love Peacock

To Cruel Ocean

Where are the hapless shipmen?—disappeared,
Gone down, where witness none, save Night, hath been,
Ye deep, deep waves, of kneeling mothers feared,
What dismal tales know ye of things unseen?
Tales that ye tell your whispering selves between
The while in clouds to the flood-tide ye pour;
And this it is that gives you, as I ween,
Those mournful voices, mournful evermore,
When ye come in at eve to us who dwell on shore.

Victor Hugo

The sea, to be happy, like hearts, must be stirred.

Will Advise, writer

My brother William is
a fisherman, and he tells
me that when he is in the
middle of a fogbound sea
the water is a colour for
which there is no name.

Patricia MacLachlan, *Sarah, Plain and Tall*

So fine was the morning except for a streak of wind here and there that the sea and sky looked all one fabric, as if sails were stuck high up in the sky, or the clouds had dropped down into the sea.

Virginia Woolf, *To the Lighthouse*

The Ayia Napa is said to live in the seas around Cyprus. Unlike most sea monsters, it's said to be friendly. Descriptions of the creature vary from a multi-headed sea serpent to a giant crocodile.

The Pacific is my home ocean; I knew it first, grew up on its shore, collected marine animals along the coast. I know its moods, its colour, its nature. It was very far inland that I caught the first smell of the Pacific. When one has been long at sea, the smell of land reaches far out to greet one. And the same it true when one has been long inland.

John Steinbeck, *Travels with Charley*

The breaking of a
wave cannot explain
the whole sea.

Vladimir Nabokov, writer

It isn't always the treasure that drives men down deep into the sea; it's something else, something unexplainable, even to them.

Jennifer Arnett, *Into Her Chambers*

By the Sea

Why does the sea moan evermore?
Shut out from heaven it makes its moan,
It frets against the boundary shore;
All earth's full rivers cannot fill
The sea, that drinking thirsteth still.

Sheer miracles of loveliness
Lie hid in its unlooked-on bed:
Anemones, salt, passionless,
Blow flower-like; just enough alive
To blow and multiply and thrive.

Shells quaint with curve, or spot, or spike,
Encrusted live things argus-eyed,
All fair alike, yet all unlike,
Are born without a pang, and die
Without a pang, and so pass by.

Christina Rossetti

The earth requires the use of its two-thirds water to keep its face clean.

James Lendall Basford, *Seven Seventy Seven Sensations*

from "Ocean"

I will no more sail upon an ocean,
For it fills my heart with strange emotion.

Bernard Shaw

The sea is everything. It covers seven-tenths of the terrestrial globe. Its breath is pure and healthy. It is an immense desert, where man is never lonely, for he feels life stirring on all sides. The sea is only the embodiment of a supernatural and wonderful existence. It is nothing but love and emotion; it is the "Living Infinite", as one of your poets has said... The sea does not belong to despots. Upon its surface men can still exercise unjust laws, fight, tear one another to pieces, and be carried away with terrestrial horrors. But at thirty feet below its level, their reign ceases, their influence is quenched, and their power disappears. Ah! sir, live—live in the bosom of the waters! There only is independence! There I recognise no masters! There I am free!

Jules Verne, *20,000 Leagues Under the Sea*

Ocean sailing does not cease at sunset, or when a motel is reached, or when one is tired of it. It goes on and on, day and night, hour after hour, seasickness and discomfort notwithstanding, hammering seas be damned.

Tom Wicker, *Rough Passage*

Both Asian and Native American tribes have legends of creatures that are part-human, part-octopus.

The Atlantic is the second largest ocean in the world, and covers about 21 percent of the planet's surface.

All rivers do their best for the sea.

Czech Proverb

I felt the full breadth and depth of the ocean around the sphere of the Earth, back billions of years to the beginning of life, across all the passing lives and deaths, the endless waves of swimming joy and quiet losses of exquisite creatures with fins and fronds, tentacles and wings, colourful and transparent, tiny and huge, coming and going. There is nothing the ocean has not seen.

Sally Andrew, *The Fire Dogs of Climate Change: An Inspirational Call to Action*

from "The Triumph of the Whale"

Io! Pæan! Io! sing
To the finny people's King.
Not a mightier whale than this
In the vast Atlantic is;
Not a fatter fish than he
Flounders round the polar sea.
See his blubbers-at his gills
What a world of drink he swills,
From his trunk, as from a spout,
Which next moment he pours out.
Such his person-next declare,
Muse, who his companions are.-
Every fish of generous kind
Scuds aside, or slinks behind;
But about his presence keep
All the Monsters of the Deep;
Mermaids, with their tails and singing.
His delighted fancy stinging;
Crooked Dolphins, they surround him,
Dog-like Seals, they fawn around him.

Charles Lamb

The famous "seven seas" are the Arctic, Antarctic, North Pacific, South Pacific, North Atlantic, South Atlantic and Indian Oceans.

Whales sing because they love the feel of the ocean against their skin.

Anthony T. Hincks, writer

All is going on as it was wont. The waves are hoarse with repetition of their mystery; the dust lies piled upon the shore; the sea-birds soar and hover; the winds and clouds go forth upon their trackless flight; the white arms beckon, in the moonlight, to the invisible country far away.

Charles Dickens, *Dombey and Son*

Many medieval bestiaries feature a creature called Aspidochelone, a sea turtle so enormous that sailors mistake it for an island.

Never seen the sea!
How could anyone not
have seen the sea?
Surely the sea must
somehow belong to the
happiness of every child.

Iris Murdoch, *The Time of the Angels*

He held it indeed as certain, that no person, [...] could be really in a state of secure and permanent Health without spending at least six weeks by the Sea every year.

Jane Austen, *Sanditon*

From "maggie and milly and molly and may"

for whatever we lose (like a you or a me),
it's always our self we find in the sea.

e.e. cummings

On the Sea

It keeps eternal whisperings around
Desolate shores, and with its mighty swell
Gluts twice ten thousand Caverns, till the spell
Of Hecate leaves them their old shadowy sound.
Often 'tis in such gentle temper found,
That scarcely will the very smallest shell
Be moved for days from where it sometime fell.
When last the winds of Heaven were unbound.
Oh, ye! who have your eyeballs vexed and tired,
Feast them upon the wideness of the Sea;
Oh ye! whose ears are dinned with uproar rude,
Or fed too much with cloying melody—
Sit ye near some old Cavern's Mouth and brood,
Until ye start, as if the sea nymphs quired!

John Keats

The ocean is a place of skin,
rich outer membranes
hiding thick juicy insides,
laden with the soup of being.

Vera Nazarian,
The Perpetual Calendar of Inspiration

There are about 229,000 known species
in the ocean. Scientists estimate
that up to two million more may be
awaiting discovery.

Be alone with the sea for it is there you will find answers to questions you didn't realize existed.

Khang Kijarro Nguyen, artist

The moon went slowly down in loveliness; she departed into the depth of the horizon, and long veil-like shadows crept up the sky through which the stars appeared. Soon, however, they too began to pale before a splendour in the east, and the advent of the dawn declared itself in the newborn blue of heaven. Quieter and yet more quiet grew the sea, quiet as the soft mist that brooded on her bosom, and covered up her troubling, as in our tempestuous life the transitory wreaths of sleep brook upon a pain-racked soul, causing it to forget its sorrow. From the east to the west sped those angels of the Dawn, from sea to sea, from mountain-top to mountain-top, scattering light from breast and wing.

H. Rider Haggard, *She: A History of Adventure*

You have to understand the sea, he said, to listen to her, to look out for her moods, to get to know her and respect her and love her. Only then can you build boats that feel at home on the sea.

Michael Morpurgo, *Alone on a Wide Wide Sea*

from "By the Sea"

Beside an ebbing northern sea
While stars awaken one by one,
We walk together, I and he.

Sara Teasdale

The heart is but
the beach beside
the sea that is
the world.

Chinese Proverb

Many countries and religions have legends concerning giant sea creatures that swallow humans who are later freed. The two most famous examples are Jonah from the Bible and the Rainbow Fish that was said to have held Buddha in its stomach until the fish was caught and Buddha was cut free.

The sea always makes me watch it all the time. I've spent hours and hours not just on the sea but just watching wave after wave come in. If it's an image of anything, I think it's an image of our own unconscious, the unconscious of our own minds... or you can put it the other way around, and that is that we have a sea in us. After all, we are sea creatures that learned to walk on the land, are we not? And perhaps one way or another we go back to it. Every night when we dream we go back into that kind of depths, and that kind of beauty and monstrosity and mystery. So really the sea is not a single image, it can really image almost anything that the human mind can discover.

William Golding, writer

One of the most famous maritime legends is that of Atlantis, a huge island that is supposed to have sunk into the water after its people became arrogant and angered the gods.

*n*owhere else than upon the sea do the days, weeks and months fall away quicker into the past.

Joseph Conrad,
The Mirror of the Sea

The longest mountain range in the world is found under water. The Mid-Oceanic Ridge is a chain that runs more than 56,000 kilometres (34,800 miles) around the globe.

The ocean exerts an inexorable pull over sea people wherever they are—in a bright-lit, inland city or the dead centre of a desert—and when they feel the tug there is no choice but somehow to reach it and stand at its immense, earth-dissolving edge, straightaway calmed.

Anuradha Roy, *The Folded Earth*

Long before we saw the sea, its spray was on our lips, and showered salt rain upon us.

Charles Dickens, *David Copperfield*

And then, the unspeakable purity – and freshness of the air! There was just enough heat to enhance the value of the breeze, and just enough wind to keep the whole sea in motion, to make the waves come bounding to the shore, foaming and sparkling, as if wild with glee.

Anne Brontë, *Agnes Grey*

He was sailing over a boundless expanse of sea, with a blood-red sky above, and the angry waters, lashed into fury beneath, boiling and eddying up, on every side. There was another vessel before them, toiling and labouring in the howling storm: her canvas fluttering in ribbons from the mast.

Charles Dickens, *The Pickwick Papers*

The waves of the
sea help me get
back to me.

Jill Davis, writer

Waves are the practice of water. To speak of waves apart from water, or water apart from waves, is a delusion.

Shunryū Suzuki, monk

from "The Sea"

I love, O, how I love to ride
On the fierce, foaming, bursting tide,
When every mad wave drowns the moon
Or whistles aloft his tempest tune,
And tells how goeth the world below,
And why the sou'west blasts do blow.

I never was on the dull, tame shore,
But I lov'd the great sea more and more,
And backwards flew to her billowy breast,
Like a bird that seeketh its mother's nest;
And a mother she was, and is, to me;
For I was born on the open sea!
The waves were white, and red the morn,

In the noisy hour when I was born;
And the whale it whistled, the porpoise roll'd,
And the dolphins bared their backs of gold;
And never was heard such an outcry wild
As welcom'd to life the ocean-child!

I've liv'd since then, in calm and strife,
Full fifty summers, a sailor's life,
With wealth to spend and a power to range,
But never have sought nor sighed for change;
And Death, whenever he comes to me,
Shall come on the wild, unbounded sea!

Barry Cornwall

This morning, one of our companie looking over board saw a mermaid, and calling up some of the companie to see her, one more came up, and by that time shee was come close to the ship's side, looking earnestly on the men: a little after, a sea came and overturned her: from the navill upward, her backe and breasts were like a woman's... her body as big as one of us; her skin very white; and long haire hanging downe behinde, of colour black; in her going down they saw her tayle, which was like the tayle of a porposse, and speckled like a macrell.

Henry Hudson, ship's log of the *Hopewell*, sailing in the Barents Sea on 15 June, 1608

All rivers run to the sea,
yet the sea is not full.

Solomon, King of Israel

The Ocean Said to Me Once

The ocean said to me once,
"Look!
Yonder on the shore
Is a woman, weeping.
I have watched her.
Go you and tell her this —
Her lover I have laid
In cool green hall.
There is wealth of golden sand
And pillars, coral-red;
Two white fish stand guard at his bier.

"Tell her this
And more —
That the king of the seas
Weeps too, old, helpless man.
The bustling fates
Heap his hands with corpses
Until he stands like a child
With a surplus of toys."

Stephen Crane

The sea is at its best at London, near midnight, when you are within the arms of a capacious chair, before a glowing fire, selecting phases of the voyages you will never make.

H. M. Tomlinson, *The Sea and the Jungle*

The sigh of all the seas breaking in measure round the isles soothed them; the night wrapped them; nothing broke their sleep, until, the birds beginning and the dawn weaving their thin voices in to its whiteness.

Virginia Woolf, *To the Lighthouse*

I sometimes think my vision of the sea
is the clearest thing I own. I pick it up,
exile that I am, like the purple "lucky
stones" I used to collect with a white
ring all the way round, or the shell of a
blue mussel with its rainbowy angel's
fingernail interior; and in one wash of
memory the colours deepen and gleam,
the early world draws breath.

Sylvia Plath, *Ocean 1212-W*

At the Sea-Side

When I was down beside the sea
A wooden spade they gave to me
To dig the sandy shore.

My holes were empty like a cup.
In every hole the sea came up,
Till it could come no more.

Robert Louis Stevenson

After a visit to the beach, it's hard to believe that we live in a material world.

Pam Shaw, motivational speaker

The deepest part of the ocean is the Challenger Deep, part of the Mariana Trench in the Pacific Ocean. It is approximately 11,033 metres (36,200 feet) deep.

By the Sea

I started early, took my dog,
And visited the sea;
The mermaids in the basement
Came out to look at me.

And frigates in the upper floor
Extended hempen hands,
Presuming me to be a mouse
Aground, upon the sands.

But no man moved me till the tide
Went past my simple shoe,
And past my apron and my belt,
And past my bodice too,

And made as he would eat me up
As wholly as a dew
Upon a dandelion's sleeve –
And then I started too.

And he – he followed close behind;
I felt his silver heel
Upon my ankle, – then my shoes
Would overflow with pearl.

Until we met the solid town,
No man he seemed to know;
And bowing with a mighty look
At me, the sea withdrew.

Emily Dickinson

The sea, like a crinkled
chart, spread to the
horizon, and lapped
the sharp outline of the
coast, while the houses
were white shells in a
rounded grotto, pricked
here and there by a
great orange sun.

Daphne du Maurier, *Rebecca*

The Chinese goddess of the sea, Mazu, is based on a real historical figure. Lin Mo was a Fujianese shamaness who lived from circa 960 to circa 987 CE. Mazu is thought to travel throughout the seas, watching over sailors and their ships.

The sea answers all questions, and always in the same way; for when you read in the papers the interminable discussions and the bickering and the prognostications and the turmoil, the disagreements and the fateful decisions and agreements and the plans and the programs and the threats and the counter threats, then you close your eyes and the sea dispatches one more big roller in the unbroken line since the beginning of the world and it combs and breaks and returns foaming and saying: "So soon?"

E. B. White, *On A Florida Key*

The Klabautermann was a kind of spirit that lived aboard ships in the Baltic and the North Sea, and helped fishermen with their duties, and rescued them if they fell overboard. A carved image of a Klabautermann, dressed in yellow with a pipe and a sailor's cap was often attached to the mast by good luck. But no sailor hoped to catch a glimpse of the real thing: if he became visible, it meant the ship was doomed.

In still moments by the sea
life seems large-drawn and
simple. It is there we can see
into ourselves.

Rolf Edberg, journalist

The world's finest
wilderness lies
beneath the waves.

Wyland, artist

from "Long Trip"

The sea is a desert of waves,
A wilderness of water.

Langston Hughes

He loved the sea for deep-seated reasons: the hardworking artist's need for repose, the desire to take shelter from the demanding diversity of phenomena in the bosom of boundless simplicity, a propensity—proscribed and diametrically opposed to his mission in life and for that very reason seductive—a propensity for the unarticulated, the immoderate, the eternal, for nothingness. To repose in perfection is the desire of all those who strive for excellence, and is not nothingness a form of perfection?

Thomas Mann, *Death in Venice*

The Ancient Greeks believed that sea nymphs called Sirens lived on an island in the Mediterranean Sea and sang enchanted songs to passing sailors, luring them to their deaths.

By the Seaside

The sun is couched, the sea-fowl gone to rest,
And the wild storm hath somewhere found a nest;
Air slumbers—wave with wave no longer strives,
Only a heaving of the deep survives,
A tell-tale motion! soon will it be laid,
And by the tide alone the water swayed.
Stealthy withdrawings, interminglings mild
Of light with shade in beauty reconciled—
Such is the prospect far as sight can range,
The soothing recompence, the welcome change.
Where, now, the ships that drove before the blast,
Threatened by angry breakers as they passed;
And by a train of flying clouds bemocked;
Or, in the hollow surge, at anchor rocked
As on a bed of death? Some lodge in peace,
Saved by His care who bade the tempest cease;
And some, too heedless of past danger, court
Fresh gales to waft them to the far-off port.

William Wordsworth

There was a magic about the sea. People were drawn to it. People wanted to love by it, swim in it, play in it, look at it. It was a living thing that was as unpredictable as a great stage actor: it could be calm and welcoming, opening its arms to embrace it's audience one moment, but then could explode with its stormy tempers, flinging people around, wanting them out, attacking coastlines, breaking down islands.

Cecelia Ahern, *The Gift*

The Ancient Greeks
believed that sea nymphs
called Sirens lived
on an island in the
Mediterranean Sea and
sang enchanted songs to
passing sailors, luring them
to their deaths.

Who that has ever visited the borders of this classic sea, has not felt at the first sight of its waters a glow of reverent rapture akin to devotion, and an instinctive sensation of thanksgiving at being permitted to stand before these hallowed waves? All that concerns the Mediterranean is of the deepest interest to civilized man, for the history of its progress is the history of the development of the world; the memory of the great men who have lived and died around its banks; the recollection of the undying works that have come thence to delight us for ever; the story of patient research and brilliant discoveries connected with every physical phenomenon presented by its waves and currents, and with every order of creatures dwelling in and around its waters. The science of the Mediterranean is the epitome of the science of the world.

Edward Forbes, *The Natural History of the European Seas*

I love the beach. I love the sea. All my life I live within – in front of the sea.

Rafael Nadal,
professional tennis player

All loose things seem
to drift down to the
sea, and so did I.

Louis L'Amour

According to NASA,
there are about
620,000 kilometres
(372,000 miles) of
coastline on Earth.

The sea is emotion incarnate. It loves, hates, and weeps. It defies all attempts to capture it with words and rejects all shackles. No matter what you say about it, there is always that which you can't.

Christopher Paolini, *Eragon*

The sea will grant each man
new hope, and sleep will
bring dreams of home…

Christopher Columbus, explorer

from "Dover Beach"

The sea is calm tonight.
The tide is full, the moon lies fair
Upon the straits; on the French coast the light
Gleams and is gone; the cliffs of England stand,
Glimmering and vast, out in the tranquil bay.
Come to the window, sweet is the night-air!
Only, from the long line of spray
Where the sea meets the moon-blanched land,
Listen! you hear the grating roar
Of pebbles which the waves draw back, and
fling,
At their return, up the high strand,
Begin, and cease, and then again begin,
With tremulous cadence slow, and bring
The eternal note of sadness in.

Matthew Arnold

Ocean is more ancient
than the mountains,
and freighted with
the memories and the
dreams of Time.

H. P. Lovecraft, *The White Ship*

There are waterfalls in the ocean. The Denmark Strait cataract between Greenland and Iceland carries 5 million cubic metres (175 million cubic feet) of water down 3,500 metres (11,500 feet). The waterfall is formed by the temperature difference between the water on each side of the strait. When the colder, denser water from the east meets the warmer, lighter water from the west, the cold water flows down and underneath the warm water. The Denmark Strait cataract is more than three times the height of Angel Falls in Venezuela, and carries almost 2,000 times the amount of water of Niagara Falls.

The oceans contain 99 percent of the living space on our planet.

They walked, and the long waves rolled
and murmured rhythmically beside
them; the fresh salty wind blew free and
unobstructed in their faces, wrapped
itself around their ears, and made them
feel slightly numb and deliciously dizzy.
They walked along in that wide, peaceful,
whispering hush of the sea that gives
every sound, near or far, some mysterious
importance.

Thomas Mann, *Buddenbrooks*

[The sea] contains so many colours. Silver at dawn, green at noon, dark blue in the evening. Sometimes it looks almost red. Or it will turn the colour of old coins. Right now the shadows of clouds are dragging across it, and patches of sunlight are touching down everywhere. White strings of gulls drag over it like beads.

Anthony Doerr, *All the Light We Cannot See*

The Roman god of the ocean was known as Neptune, and he was acknowledged for victories in battles at sea.

I preferred to look at the sea,
which said nothing and never
made you feel alone.

Paula McLain, *The Paris Wife*

The three great elemental sounds in nature are the sound of rain, the sound of wind in a primeval wood, and the sound of outer ocean on a beach. I have heard them all, and of the three elemental voices, that of ocean is the most awesome, beautiful and varied.

Henry Beston, *The Outermost House: A Year of Life on the Great Beach of Cape Cod*

I am not a religious man per se. My own cosmology is convoluted and not in line with any particular church or philosophy. But for me, to go to sea is to glimpse the face of God. At sea I am reminded of my insignificance, of all men's insignificance. It is a wonderful feeling to be so humbled.

Steve Callahan, sailor

A lot of people attack the sea, I make love to it.

Jacques-Yves Cousteau, oceanographer

The Great Barrier Reef is the world's biggest coral reef, and can be seen from space.

As far as we know, our oceans are unique in the universe. No other planet in our solar system has large bodies of liquid water on its surface. Scientists think that planets in other solar systems may have oceans, but there is as yet no proof.

I spin on the circle of
wave upon wave of the
sea, the sea's university.

Pablo Neruda, *The Sea*

The Celtic sea god Manannán mac Lir appears in many myths and legends. He is said to protect the Isle of Man from invaders by shrouding it in impenetrable fog.

To me, the sea is like a person, like a child that I've known a long time. It sounds crazy, I know, but when I swim in the sea I talk to it. I never feel alone when I'm out there.

Gertrude Ederle, first woman to swim the English Channel

from "The Ocean"

Of coral rocks, from waves below
In steep ascent that tower,
And fraught with peril, daily grow,
Formed by an insect's power;

Of sea-fires, which at dead of night
Shine o'er the tides afar,
And make th' expanse of ocean bright
As heaven, with many a star.

Oh God! thy name they well may praise,
Who to the deep go down,
And trace the wonders of thy ways,
Where rocks and billows frown.

If glorious be that awful deep,
No human power can bind,
What then art Thou, who bidst it keep
Within its bounds confined!

Let heaven and earth in praise unite,
Eternal praise to Thee,
Whose word can rouse the tempest's might,
Or still the raging sea!

Felicia Dorothea Hemans

Land was created to provide a place for boats to visit.

Brooks Atkinson, theatre critic

from "The Tempest"

Full fathom five thy father lies;
Of his bones are coral made;
Those are pearls that were his eyes:
Nothing of him that doth fade,
But doth suffer a sea-change
Into something rich and strange.
Sea-nymphs hourly ring his knell:
                    Ding-dong.
Hark! now I hear them,—ding-dong, bell.

William Shakespeare

We clear the harbor and the wind catches her sails and my beautiful ship leans over ever so gracefully, and her elegant bow cuts cleanly into the increasing chop of the waves. I take a deep breath and my chest expands and my heart starts thumping so strongly I fear the others might see it beat through the cloth of my jacket. I face the wind and my lips peel back from my teeth in a grin of pure joy.

L. A. Meyer, *Under the Jolly Roger*

Out of sight of land the sailor feels safe. It is the beach that worries him.

Charles G. Davis

from "On the Power of Sound"

The ocean is a mighty harmonist.

William Wordsworth

And oh, the cry of the seagulls! Have you ever heard it? Can you remember?

C. S. Lewis, *The Lion, the Witch and the Wardrobe*

Break, Break, Break!

Break, break, break,
On thy cold gray stones, O Sea!
And I would that my tongue could utter
The thoughts that arise in me.

O, well for the fisherman's boy,
That he shouts with his sister at play!
O, well for the sailor lad,
That he sings in his boat on the bay!

And the stately ships go on
To their haven under the hill;
But O for the touch of a vanished hand,
And the sound of a voice that is still!

Break, break, break,
At the foot of thy crags, O Sea!
But the tender grace of a day that is dead
Will never come back to me.

Alfred Lord Tennyson

If you want to build
a ship, don't drum up
people together to collect
wood and don't assign
them tasks and work,
but rather teach them
to long for the endless
immensity of the sea.

Antoine de Saint-Exupéry, *The Wisdom of the Sands*

The use of sea and air is common to all; neither can a title to the ocean belong to any people or private persons, forasmuch as neither nature nor public use and custom permit any possession thereof.

Elizabeth I, Queen of England

from "Miracles"

To me the sea is a continual miracle.
The fishes that swim—the rocks—the motion of the waves—the ships with men in them,
What stranger miracles are there?

Walt Whitman

What would an ocean be without
a monster lurking in the dark?
It would be like sleep without dreams.

Werner Herzog, screenwriter

Mid-ocean in War-time

The fragile splendour of the level sea,
The moon's serene and silver-veiled face,
Make of this vessel an enchanted place
Full of white mirth and golden sorcery.
Now, for a time, shall careless laughter be
Blended with song, to lend song sweeter grace,
And the old stars, in their unending race,
Shall heed and envy young humanity.
And yet to-night, a hundred leagues away,
These waters blush a strange and awful red.
Before the moon, a cloud obscenely grey
Rises from decks that crash with flying lead.
And these stars smile their immemorial way
On waves that shroud a thousand newly dead!

Joyce Kilmer

from "The Amber Whale"

WE were down in the Indian Ocean, after sperm, and three years out;
The last six months in the tropics, and looking in vain for a spout,—
Five men up on the royal yards, weary of straining their sight;
And every day like its brother,—just morning and noon and night—
Nothing to break the sameness: water and wind and sun
Motionless, gentle, and blazing,—never a change in one.
Every day like its brother: when the noonday eight-bells came,
'Twas like yesterday; and we seemed to know that to-morrow would be the same.
The foremast hands had a lazy time: there was never a thing to do;
The ship was painted, tarred down, and scraped; and the mates had nothing new.
We'd worked at sinnet and ratline till there wasn't a yarn to use,
And all we could do was watch and pray for a sperm whale's spout—or news.

John Boyle O'Reilly

There is pleasure in the
pathless woods, there
is rapture in the lonely
shore, there is society
where none intrudes,
by the deep sea, and
music in its roar. I love
not Man the less, but
Nature more.

Lord Byron, poet

$\mathcal{M}$arine organisms do not care about international boundaries; they move where they will.

Paul Snelgrove, oceanographer

Mid-ocean in War-time

The fragile splendour of the level sea,
The moon's serene and silver-veiled face,
Make of this vessel an enchanted place
Full of white mirth and golden sorcery.
Now, for a time, shall careless laughter be
Blended with song, to lend song sweeter grace,
And the old stars, in their unending race,
Shall heed and envy young humanity.
And yet to-night, a hundred leagues away,
These waters blush a strange and awful red.
Before the moon, a cloud obscenely grey
Rises from decks that crash with flying lead.
And these stars smile their immemorial way
On waves that shroud a thousand newly dead!

Joyce Kilmer

The old man knew he was
going far out and he left
the smell of the land behind
and rowed out into the
clean early morning smell of
the ocean.

Ernest Hemingway, *The Old Man and the Sea*

Surely we have a responsibility to care for our blue planet. The future of humanity, and indeed all life on Earth, now depends on us.

Sir David Attenborough, broadcaster

No matter how big the sea may be, sometimes two ships meet.

Chinese Proverb

People ask: "Why should I care about the ocean? Because the ocean is the cornerstone of earth's life support system, it shapes climate and weather. It holds most of life on earth. 97 per cent of earth's water is there. It's the blue heart of the planet—we should take care of our heart. It's what makes life possible for us. We still have a really good chance to make things better than they are. They won't get better unless we take the action and inspire others to do the same thing. No one is without power. Everybody has the capacity to do something."

Sylvia Earle, *The World is Blue: How Our Fate and the Oceans are One*

The sea drives truth
into a man like salt.

Hilaire Belloc, writer

from "North Sea off Carnoustie"

The sea is as near as we come to another world.

Anne Stevenson

Moon and Sea

You are the moon, dear love, and I the sea:
The tide of hope swells high within my breast,
And hides the rough dark rocks of life's unrest
When your fond eyes smile near in perigee.
But when that looking face is turned from me,
Low falls the tide, and the grim rocks appear,
And earth's dim coast-line seems a thing to fear.
You are the moon, dear one, and I the sea.

Ella Wheeler Wilcox

The waves glowed like lava, and I imagined I could see multitudes of living beings – algae, whales, sea monsters – reveling in an orgy, from the surface to the bottom of the sea. Immortality was the law here. The whole planet raged with animation. At times, I heard my name in the clamor: the spirit of the abyss calling me to join them in their nocturnal dance.

Isaac Bashevis Singer, writer

Christopher Columbus claimed to have seen three mermaids on his first voyage to the Americas in 1493. It is thought that in reality they were manatees.

The sea is one rare wild card left in the homogenous suburban life.

Tim Winton, *Land's Edge*

The myth of Atlantis is not the only one to tell of a sunken continent. The continent of Lemuria was once believed to have existed in the Pacific Ocean, and many Darwinian scientists thought that it might contain the missing link fossil records on the origin of the human species. However, recently discoveries about plate tectonics have discredited the Lemuria theory entirely.

from "The Consecrating Mother"

I stand before the sea
and it rolls and rolls in its green blood
saying, "Do not give up one god
for I have a handful."

Anne Sexton

from *The Lord of the Rings*

To the Sea, to the Sea! The white gulls are crying,
The wind is blowing, and the white foam is flying.
West, west away, the round sun is falling.
Grey ship, grey ship, do you hear them calling.
The voices of my people that have gone before me?

J. R. R. Tolkien

When we came within sight of the sea, the waves on the horizon, caught at intervals above the rolling abyss, were like glimpses of another shore with towers and buildings.

Charles Dickens, *David Copperfield*

The sea, he thought, had treasured its memories deeper than the faithless land.

F. Scott Fitzgerald, *This Side of Paradise*

Sonnet to Ocean

Shall I rebuke thee, Ocean, my old love,
That once, in rage, with the wild winds at strife,
Thou darest menace my unit of a life,
Sending my clay below, my soul above,
Whilst roar'd thy waves, like lions when they rove
By night, and bound upon their prey by stealth!
Yet didst thou n'er restore my fainting health?—
Didst thou ne'er murmur gently like the dove?
Nay, dost thou not against my own dear shore
Full break, last link between my land and me?—
My absent friends talk in thy very roar,
In thy waves' beat their kindly pulse I see,
And, if I must not see my England more,
Next to her soil, my grave be found in thee!

Thomas Hood

There is, one knows not what sweet mystery about this sea, whose gently awful stirrings seem to speak of some hidden soul beneath; like those fabled undulations of the Ephesian sod over the buried Evangelist St. John. And meet it is, that over these sea-pastures, wide-rolling watery prairies and Potters' Fields of all four continents, the waves should rise and fall, and ebb and flow unceasingly; for here, millions of mixed shades and shadows, drowned dreams, somnambulisms, reveries; all that we call lives and souls, lie dreaming, dreaming, still; tossing like slumberers in their beds; the ever-rolling waves but made so by their restlessness.

Herman Melville, *Moby Dick*

The Ancient Greek god of the sea was known as Poseidon. After the fall of the Titans, he and his brothers drew lots for the division of the cosmos, and he won the sea as his domain.

At sea, I learned how little a person
needs, not how much.

Robin Lee Graham, sailor

There are lakes at the bottom
of the ocean! The proportion of
salt in seawater is not always
consistent, and particularly
salty water will sink, forming
pools and even rivers, with
distinct shorelines.

It is a curious situation that the sea, from which life first arose should now be threatened by the activities of one form of that life. But the sea, though changed in a sinister way, will continue to exist; the threat is rather to life itself.

Rachel Carson, *The Sea Around Us*

All of us have, in our veins the exact same percentage of salt in our blood that exists in the ocean, and, therefore, we have salt in our blood, in our sweat, in our tears. We are tied to the ocean. And when we go back to the sea, whether it is to sail or to watch it we are going back from whence we came.

John F. Kennedy, former US President

"Waves are the voices of tides. Tides are life," murmured Niko. "They bring new food for shore creatures, and take ships out to sea. They are the ocean's pulse, and our own heartbeat."

Tamora Pierce, *Sandry's Book*

Time is more complex near the
sea than in any other place, for in
addition to the circling of the sun
and the turning of the seasons, the
waves beat out the passage of time
on the rocks and the tides rise and
fall as a great clepsydra.

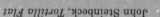
John Steinbeck, *Tortilla Flat*

The Fijian god Takuaka is said to be able to change into a shark so he can travel from island to island, challenging their guardians to battle.

from "On the Seas and Far Away"

How can my poor heart be glad,
When absent from my sailor lad;
How can I the thought forego,
He's on the seas to meet the foe?
Let me wander, let me rove,
Still my heart is with my love;
Nightly dreams, and thoughts by day,
Are with him that's far away.

[Chorus]
On the seas and far away,
On stormy seas and far away;
Nightly dreams and thoughts by day,
Are aye with him that's far away.

Robert Burns

When you finally see what goes on underwater, you realize that you've been missing the whole point of the ocean. Staying on the surface all the time is like going to the circus and staring at the outside of the tent.

Dave Barry, newspaper columnist

The world record for deepest scuba dive was set in 2014 by Egyptian Ahmed Gabr, who descended 332 metres (1,090 feet) into the Red Sea. It took him twelve minutes to get down there – and fourteen minutes to return safely.

There is no competing with the sea in a man's affections, since she is both mother and mistress, and she will wash his corpse also, in time to come, wash it to coral and ivory and pearls.

Neil Gaiman, *Stardust*

from "If I Should Have a Daughter"

Because there's nothing more beautiful than the way the ocean refuses to stop kissing the shoreline, no matter how many times it's sent away.

Sarah Kay

"Song of the Sea"

Timeless sea breezes,
sea-wind of the night:
you come for no one;
if someone should wake,
he must be prepared
how to survive you.
Timeless sea breezes,
that for aeons have
blown ancient rocks,
you are purest space
coming from afar…
Oh, how a fruit-bearing
fig tree feels your coming
high up in the moonlight.

Rainer Maria Rilke

The octopus had four tentacles that floated on the surface of the water, while the other four grasped the reef. When Takuaka tried to attack, the floating tentacles wrapped around him and squeezed him almost to death. For the first time ever, Takuaka admitted defeat. He begged the octopus to let him go and he would never harm humans again.

If the private life of the sea could ever be transposed onto paper, it would talk not about rivers or rain or glaciers or of molecules of oxygen and hydrogen, but of the millions of encounters its waters have shared with creatures of another nature.

Federico Chini, *The Sea of Forgotten Memories*

from "The Sea is History"

Where are your monuments, your battles, martyrs?
Where is your tribal memory? Sirs,
in that gray vault. The sea. The sea
has locked them up. The sea is History.

Derek Walcott

from "The Rime of the Ancient Mariner"

Water, water, everywhere,
And all the boards did shrink;
Water, water, everywhere,
Nor any drop to drink.

Samuel Taylor Coleridge

One day, Takuaka went to fight the guardian of the Kamatuwu Islands. As he approached the entrance to the reef that guarded the islands he found a huge octopus waiting for him – the guardian.

Praise the sea; on the shore remain.

John Florio, tutor at the court of James I of England

The sea has never been, and I fancy will be nor can be painted; it is only suggested by a means of more or less spiritual and intelligent conventionalism.

John Ruskin, artist

Mount Everest is famously the tallest mountain on land, but it is not as tall as the island of Mauna Kea, if the distance from the bottom of the ocean to the peak of this island is measured. Mount Everest is a mere 8,850 metres (29,000 feet), while Mauna Kea is more than 10,000 metres (32,800 feet).

"Doesn't it seem to you," asked Madame Bovary, "that the mind moves more freely in the presence of that boundless expanse, that the sight of it elevates the soul and gives rise to thoughts of the infinite and the ideal?"

Gustave Flaubert, *Madame Bovary*

There is nothing quite so good as burial at sea. It is simple, tidy, and not very incriminating.

Alfred Hitchcock, film director

The Ainu people of Japan used to hold funerals for orcas that washed ashore, believing them to be sea deities.

Sailors on old trading vessels used to have roosters and pigs tattooed on their feet. They believed the animals would save them from drowning by showing them the way to shore.

A fragrant breeze wandered up from the quiet sea, trailed along the beach, and drifted back to the sea again, wondering where to go next. On a mad impulse it went up to the beach again. It drifted back to sea.

Douglas Adams, *The Hitchhiker's Guide to the Galaxy*

The sea was as black as basalt, covered with churning foam, ice-green, clotted cream, shivering high walls full of needles of air going up and up and crashing down on other walls of water on the crumbling coasts of the world.

A. S. Byatt, *Ragnarok*

from "Address to the Ocean"

Oh! thus that your voice had still thundered!
Your arms for destruction been spread!
My Charles and I ne'er had been sundered;
But now had I pillowed his head.

The love which the waves must dissever,
The hope which the winds might deceive,
Why these, my sole stay, could I ever
Permit him this bosom to leave?

Oh! where are thy beauties, my lover?
And where is thy dark flowing hair?
Oh God! that this storm would uncover
Thy body that once was so fair!
Through regions of darkness appalling
It sunk as the hurricane whirled;
By monsters beset in its falling,
The blood of the bottomless world.

Then ocean! thou canst not uncover
The body that once was so fair;
And lost are thy beauties, my lover!
And gone is thy dark-flowing hair!
Ye waters! I hear in your roaring
A voice from your deepest abode;
New victims in anger imploring—
My hope be the mercy of God.

William Wordsworth

from "The Omnipresence of the Deity"

And Thou, vast Ocean! on whose awful face
Time's iron feet can print no ruin-trace,
By breezes lull'd, or by the storm-blasts driv'n,
Thy majesty uplifts the mind to heaven.

Robert Montgomery

I suppose because I grew up a thousand miles from the sea and missed the great age of passenger liners, I have always been subject to a romantic longing for ocean travel.

Bill Bryson, *Down Under: Travels in a Sunburned Country*

The Norse god of the sea was known as Aegir. Sailors both worshipped and feared him, because they believed he would sometimes rise to the surface to drag ships down to the depths.

It isn't that life ashore is distasteful to me. But life at sea is better.

Sir Francis Drake, naval officer

The ocean makes me feel really small and it makes me put my whole life into perspective... it humbles you and makes you feel almost like you've been baptized. I feel born again when I get out of the ocean.

Beyoncé Knowles, singer

Some 72 percent
of Earth is covered
in water, 97 percent
of which is ocean.

from "Ocean: An Ode"

In prospect wide,
The boundless tide!
Waves cease to foam, and winds to roar;
Without a breeze,
The curling seas
Dance on, in measure, to the shore.

Edward Young

The Ocean

The Ocean has its silent caves,
Deep, quiet, and alone;
Though there be fury on the waves,
Beneath them there is none.
The awful spirits of the deep
Hold their communion there;
And there are those for whom we weep,
The young, the bright, the fair.
Calmly the wearied seamen rest
Beneath their own blue sea.
The ocean solitudes are blest,
For there is purity.
The earth has guilt, the earth has care,
Unquiet are its graves;
But peaceful sleep is ever there,
Beneath the dark blue waves.

Nathaniel Hawthorne

*L*and is the secure ground of home, the sea is like life, the outside, the unknown.

Stephen Gardiner, bishop and politician

The Hindu god of the sea is Varuna. He rides a Makara, a sea monster with the head of a deer and the body of an antelope.

It must be remembered that the sea is a great breeder of friendship. Two men who have known each other for twenty years find that twenty days at sea bring them nearer than ever they were before, or else estrange them.

Gilbert Parker, *Mrs. Falchion*

from "As I Walked Out One Evening"

I'll love you till the ocean
Is folded and hung up to dry
And the seven stars go squawking
Like geese about the sky.

W. H. Auden

We know that when we protect our oceans we're protecting our future.

Bill Clinton, former US president

There is but a plank between a sailor and eternity.

Thomas Gibbons, politician

We have given different parts of the sea different names for navigation and identification, but if we are standing before the sea, there is only one whole. The Sea.

John Ajvide Lindqvist, *Harbor*

The world's largest ocean is the Pacific, which covers about 30 percent of the planet's surface.

But during those two months of fog...
the saddest and the heaviest thing
was to stand beside the sea. To be upon
the beach yourself, and see the long
waves coming in; to know that they
are long waves, but only see a piece of
them. And to hear them lifting roundly,
swelling over smooth green rocks,
plashing down in the hollow corners, but
bearing on all the same as ever, soft and
sleek and sorrowful, till their little noise
is over.

R. D. Blackmore, *Lorna Doone*

from "The Ocean Liner"

They went down to the sea in ships,
In ships they went down to the sea.
In boats hewn of oak-tree strips,
In galleys with skin-sewn sails,
In triremes, caravels, brigs—
Frail, flimsily rolling rigs—
They went down where the huge wave rips,
Where the black storm lashes and hales.
They went down to the sea in ships,
To the sounding, sorrowing sea.

Harriet Monroe

In Roman myth, the sea god Neptune was captivated by the beauty of a water nymph called Amphitrite. He fell in love and asked for her hand in marriage but she turned him down. Neptune sent a dolphin to find her, and the dolphin was able to convince her to accept Neptune's suit. As a reward, Neptune made the dolphin immortal and gave it a place in the sky as the constellation Dolphinus.

To have a huge, friendly whale willingly approach your boat and look you straight in the eye is without doubt one of the most extraordinary experiences on the planet.

Mark Carwardine, zoologist

If you live a life of make-believe, your life isn't worth anything until you do something that does challenge your reality. And to me, sailing the open ocean is a real challenge, because it's life or death.

Morgan Freeman, actor

Though all rivers flow into it,
the sea never overflows.

Chinese Proverb

I wanted freedom, open air and adventure. I found it on the sea.

Alain Gerbault, aviator and sailor

from "The Calm"

Our storm is past, and that storm's tyrannous rage,
A stupid calm, but nothing it, doth 'suage.
The fable is inverted, and far more
A block afflicts, now, than a stork before.
Storms chafe, and soon wear out themselves, or us;
In calms, Heaven laughs to see us languish thus.
As steady' as I can wish that my thoughts were,
Smooth as thy mistress' glass, or what shines there,
The sea is now; and, as the isles which we
Seek, when we can move, our ships rooted be.

John Donne

I heard silence, silence infinite as the bottom of the ocean, a silence that sealed.

Anne Spollen, *The Shape of Water*

The sea has forests, just as does the land. Huge strands of kelp up to 35 metres (115 feet) high grow in huge clusters in some temperate waters, especially along the shores of the north-eastern Pacific. The thick groves of wavy fronds provide rich pickings for herbivores, hunting grounds for carnivores and hiding places for their prey.

That the sea is one of the most beautiful and magnificent sights in Nature, all admit.

John Joly, physicist

The cure for anything is salt water:
sweat, tears or the sea.

Isak Dinesen, writer

The Aztecs dedicated five annual celebrations to Chalchiutlicue, goddess of seas and water, and her husband, Tlaloc. Priests swum in a lake imitating the movements and croaking of frogs, in the hope of bringing rain.

The sun itself was
hidden, but there was
a glitter on the horizon,
almost like the dazzle of
the crystal walls of the
Undertomb, a kind of
joyous shimmering off on
the edge of the world.
"What is that?" the girl
said, and he: "The sea."

Ursula K. Le Guin, *The Tombs of Atuan*

from "The Stowaway"

Never a ship sails out of the bay
But carries my heart as a stowaway.

Roselle Mercier Montgomery

Underwater I hear the water coming to my body, I hear the sunlight penetrating the water.

James Nestor, *Deep: Freediving, Renegade Science and What the Ocean Tells us about Ourselves*

The sea, once it casts its spell, holds one in its net of wonder forever.

Jacques-Yves Cousteau, oceanographer

When they are gay, the waves echo their gaiety; but when they are sad, then every breaker, as it rolls, seems to bring additional sadness, and to speak to us of hopelessness and of the pettiness of all our joys.

Baroness Emma Orczy,
The Scarlet Pimpernel

Deep-sea dwelling species of small animals like sea horses and crustaceans often grow to many times the size of their surface-dwelling cousins. Nobody knows the cause of this phenomenon, which is known as deep-sea gigantism.

The ocean is a place of skin,
rich outer membranes hiding
thick juicy insides, laden
with the soup of being.

Vera Nazarian, *The Perpetual Calendar of Inspiration*

When a man comes to like a sea life, he is not fit to live on land.

Samuel Johnson, writer

from "Song of Myself"

You sea! I resign myself to you also-
I guess what you mean,
I behold from the beach your crooked fingers,
I believe you refuse to go back without feeling of me.
We must have a turn together,
I undress, hurry me out of sight of the land,
Cushion me soft, rock me billowy drowse,
Dash me with amorous wet, I can repay you.

Walt Whitman

And the voices in the waves
are always whispering to
Florence, in their ceaseless
murmuring, of love — of love,
eternal and illimitable, not
bounded by the confines of
this world, or by the end
of time, but ranging still,
beyond the sea, beyond the
sky, to the invisible country
far away!

Charles Dickens, *Dombey and Son*

In Ancient Roman times, Atargatis was a beautiful and powerful priestess who fell in love with a human shepherd boy. After she became pregnant with his baby, the shepherd boy died leaving Atargatis distraught and remorseful. Following the birth of a baby girl, Semiranis, she threw herself into the Ocean to drown. Her beauty was so great that the Gods did not let her die, but changed her into a Mermaid. Not only did she become a mermaid, but a goddess of the seas. Half woman and half fish. Atargatis was depicted as having long, flowing hair like the water. She is the first mermaid.

One cannot look at the sea
without wishing for the wings
of a swallow.

Sir Richard Francis Burton, explorer

In the 4.5-billion-year history of the Earth, the continental plates have moved around, causing the continents to break up and reform many times. Prior to its break-up, all the continents of the world were fused together in a single landmass known as Pangaea – and it was surrounded by Panthalassa (from Ancient Greek, meaning "all-sea"), a single vast ocean.

In one drop of water
are found all the secrets
of all the oceans.

Kahlil Gibran, writer and philosopher

The ocean has always been a salve to my soul... the best thing for a cut or abrasion was to go swimming in salt water. Later down the road of life, I made the discovery that salt water was also good for the mental abrasions one inevitably acquires on land.

Jimmy Buffett, musician and songwriter

You can never cross the ocean
unless you have the courage
to lose sight of the shore.

André Gide, writer

A smooth sea never made skilled mariner.

English Proverb

The Sea Monk was a kind of creature caught off the Danish coast in the 1540s. It was described as looking like a monk, and being intelligent and communicative. One Sea Monk refused to eat after being captured, and died with three days.

One Sea Monk was captured and held prisoner by the Polish king. When it met some human bishops, it asked them for release. The king agreed, and the bishops made the sign of the cross over their fishy visitor and returned him to the sea.

Laurel in the Berkshires

Sea-foam
And coral! Oh, I'll
Climb the great pasture rocks
And dream me mermaid in the sun's
Gold flood.

Adelaide Crapsey

We are going toward the sea. I have swollen. I am carried away. Sometimes at night love comes up so quickly and so high, and if we have no little boat perhaps it is because we want to roll breathless under the ocean floor.

Hélène Cixous,
The Book of Prometheus

*He that will learn to pray,
let him go to sea.*

George Herbert, poet

from "Asphodel, that Greeny Flower"

But the sea
which no one tends
is also a garden.

William Carlos Williams

The sea—this truth must be confessed—has no generosity. No display of manly qualities—courage, hardihood, endurance, faithfulness—has ever been known to touch its irresponsible consciousness of power.

Joseph Conrad, *The Mirror of the Sea*

The Kraken

Below the thunders of the upper deep;
Far far beneath in the abysmal sea,
His ancient, dreamless, uninvaded sleep
The Kraken sleepeth: faintest sunlights flee
About his shadowy sides; above him swell
Huge sponges of millennial growth and height;
And far away into the sickly light,
From many a wondrous grot and secret cell
Unnumber'd and enormous polypi
Winnow with giant arms the slumbering green.
There hath he lain for ages, and will lie
Battening upon huge seaworms in his sleep,
Until the latter fire shall heat the deep;
Then once by man and angels to be seen,
In roaring he shall rise and on the surface die.

Alfred Tennyson

Earth and sky, woods and fields, lakes and rivers, the mountain and the sea, are excellent schoolmasters, and teach some of us more than we can ever learn from books.

John Lubbock, banker

Beauty of expression
is so akin to the voice
of the sea.

George Matthew Adams, columnist

The fishermen know that the sea is
dangerous and the storm terrible, but
they have never found these dangers
sufficient reason for remaining ashore.

Vincent van Gogh, painter

There, at a depth to which divers would find it difficult to descend, are caverns, haunts, and dusky mazes, where monstrous creatures multiply and destroy each other. Huge crabs devour fish and are devoured in their turn. Hideous shapes of living things, not created to be seen by human eyes wander in this twilight. Vague forms of antennae, tentacles, fins, open jaws, scales, and claws, float about there, quivering, growing larger, or decomposing and perishing in the gloom, while horrible swarms of swimming things prowl about seeking their prey.

Victor Hugo, *Toilers of the Sea*

You can't cross the sea merely by standing and staring at the water.

Rabindranath Tagore, poet

One of the most famous modern ocean legends is that of the Flying Dutchman, a ship doomed to sail forever, unable to return home. The ship was first mentioned in print by John MacDonald in his Travels in Various Parts of Europe, Asia and Africa During a Series of Thirty Years and Upward, published in 1790: "The weather was so stormy that the sailors said they saw the Flying Dutchman. The common story is that this Dutchman came to the Cape in distress of weather and wanted to get into harbor but could not get a pilot to conduct her and was lost and that ever since in very bad weather her vision appears." Reported sightings of the ship continued through the nineteenth and most of the twentieth century.

But though, to landsmen in general, the native inhabitants of the seas have ever been regarded with emotions unspeakably unsocial and repelling; though we know the sea to be an everlasting terra incognita, so that Columbus sailed over numberless unknown worlds to discover his one superficial western one; though, by vast odds, the most terrific of all mortal disasters have immemorially and indiscriminately befallen tens and hundreds of thousands of those who have gone upon the waters; though but a moment's consideration will teach that, however baby man may brag of his science and skill, and however much, in a flattering future, that science and skill may augment; yet for ever and for ever, to the crack of doom, the sea will insult and murder him, and pulverize the stateliest, stiffest frigate he can make; nevertheless, by the continual repetition of these very impressions, man has lost that sense of the full awfulness of the sea which aboriginally belongs to it."

Herman Melville, *Moby Dick*

The sea –
Something to look at
When we are angry.

Reiko Chiba, *Hiroshige's Tokaido in Prints and Poetry*

Why do we love the sea?
It is because it has
some potent power to make us
think things we like to think.

Robert Henri, painter